Apple Magic

D0360484

AMERICAN ★ COOKING ★ GUILD™

Boynton Beach, Florida

Acknowledgments
—Edited by Martina Boudreau
—Cover Design and Layout by Pearl & Associates, Inc.
—Cover Photo by Burwell and Burwell
—Typesetting and Layout by Catharine Hocker

Revised Edition 1997

ISBN 0-942320-09-3

More...Quick Recipes for Creative Cooking!
The American Cooking Guild's *Collector's Series* includes over 30 popular cooking topics such as Barbeque, Breakfast & Brunches, Chicken, Cookies, Hors d' Oeuvres, Seafood, Tea, Coffee, Pasta, Pizza, Salads, Italian and many more. Each book contains more than 50 selected recipes. For a catalog of these and many other full sized cookbooks, send $1 to the address below and a coupon will be included for $1 off your first order.

Cookbooks Make Great Premiums!
The American Cooking Guild has been the premier publisher of private label and custom cookbooks since 1981. Retailers, manufacturers, and food companies have all chosen The American Cooking Guild to publish their premium and promotional cookbooks. For further information on our special market programs, please contact the address below.

The American Cooking Guild
3600-K South Congress Avenue
Boynton Beach, FL 33426

Table of Contents

Introduction

"Not everyone has the same taste, but there's
an apple for every taste."

The pleasures of the apple are not limited to taste. There is beauty in the delicate blossoms of Spring; comfort in the shade of green leaves in Summer's heat; and delight in Autumn air filled with the sweet smell of ripening fruit. The apple brings joy in all seasons and in many forms, but to truly know the apple is to taste it.

The best way to learn about the varieties available in your area is to visit an orchard during harvesting time and pick your own. Ask your local grower and the other "apple knockers" you meet there how they use their apples. Then, improvise! I have, in many years of cooking and baking, made many things even more delicious by the addition of an apple or two.

Apples have endless potential on their own or in combination with other fruits, juices, vegetables, meat and game, beans, nuts, cheeses and spirits. Apple dishes can be plain or fancy. In this book, we have tried to give many recipes that show the apple's versatility.

Let the recipes guide you but remember that they are only the beginning; your imagination is the limit. For example, if you want a "light" mincemeat, use green tomatoes instead of beef. Try flavoring applesauce with cardamom or vanilla, or stirring apple butter into plain yogurt. Add onion and curry powder to apple-cranberry relish for a delicious chutney. Freeze apple cider into popsicles, dip apple slices into melted semisweet chocolate, add dehydrated apples to oatmeal or granola. And don't forget to add elderberry juice to your favorite apple butter recipe for a real taste treat. Cooking with apples is easy and fun—children enjoy it too, although they end up nibbling more than cooking. And no wonder.

The apple's reputation for keeping the doctor away is well deserved. Apples contain several important nutrients, and are low in calories (only 80-90 per apple). They provide fiber and pectin, which aid digestion and rid the body of toxins. Pectin also helps keep cholesterol levels in balance. Apples are high in potassium and low in sodium. Studies also indicate that eating one to three apples a day significantly reduces the incidence of colds. Headaches and other tension problems are also reduced. Best of all, apples leave our breath fresh and teeth clean.

APPLES. . .

... are naturally juicy. Add very little water when cooking, only enough to prevent applesauce from scorching

... are naturally sweet. Use little sugar, or their flavor won't be as delightful and their texture will change to mush. Sweeten applesauce after cooking, and try using honey.

... turn brown after slicing. A bit of lemon juice wil help prevent this. Cortland and Golden Delicious apples retain their whiteness longest, so use these for salads.

... must be kept at 32°-40°. Store in plastic bags or in the refrigerator hydrator. If stored in a cellar or outdoors, wrap apples individually in newsprint and cover with a blanket to prevent freezing.

... bruise easily. Handle with care. And don't buy bruised apples— they spoil quickly.

... if immature, with a dark green "ground" or undercast, they will be starchy and hard.

... if overripe, with a dull yellowish "ground", will have poor flavor and a soft, mealy texture.

... have frequently been sprayed for insects. Wash apples with a mild soap and rinse thoroughly before eating.

... cider is best made from three to five apple varieties, some sweet, and some tart. Cider can be frozen for year-round enjoyment.

... can be stored by preparing fruit as you would for canning, using a light syrup. Rather than processing after packing, simply freeze.

... by the pound = 4 small, 3 medium, or 2 large and yield: 3 cups diced, or 2¾ cups pared and sliced, or 1½ cups shredded.

... make attractive candle holders. Remove core, except for near the base. Insert a candle.

... brighten dulled aluminum pans by boiling apple peelings in them.

... will help keep cookies soft, if a cut apple is placed in the cookie jar.

Remember to always brush your teeth after eating, especially after eating sweets. If that isn't possible... Eat An Apple!

—The Editor

Apple Facts

Variety	Appearance	Characteristics	Area Available	Season	Bake	Eat	Pie	Salad	Sauce	Preserve & Jelly
Baldwin	Red w/yellow pores	Moderately tart	Northeast, Northern Midwest	Nov-April	x	x	x		x	
Cortland	Red w/golden blush	Sweet, juicy, white flesh	Northeast	Sept-April		x	x	x	x	
Delicious	Bright red	sweet, juicy, mild	All	Sept-April		x			x	
Golden Delicious	Golden, mottled w/russet	Sweet, aromatic	All	Sept-April		x			x	x	x
Grimes Golden	Yellow dotted w/russet	Firm, crisp, aromatic, sweet	Virginia	Sept	x	x	x	x	x	
Granny Smith	Bright green	Firm, tart, juicy	California, New Zealand	June-Sept	x	x	x		x	
Gravenstein	Golden w/red stripes	Tart, spicy, firm	California	Aug-Sept	x		x		x	x
Greening	Light green	Rich, tart, crisp	New York	Oct-Feb	x		x		x	
Haralson	Red, some gold highlights	Firm, sweet, juicy	Minnesota	Sept	x	x	x			x
Jonathan	Bright red, lightly speckled	Crisp, juicy, slightly tart	Michigan, Midwest Appalachia	Aug-Jan		x	x	x	x	
Lady-tiny	Pale yellow, glossy	Firm, sweet, white flesh	Mid Atlantic	Nov-Dec		x				x
McIntosh	Two-tone red and green	Crisp, juicy, aromatic	N.E. and Midwest	Sept-Feb		x	x	x	x	
Mutsu	Yellow	Tender, fragrant	Japan	Nov-Jan	x	x			x	
Newtown Pippin	Yellow-green/ blushing pink	Firm, mildly tart	West Coast	Oct-April		x	x		x	
Rome Beauty	Red and red striped	Mild, juicy	All	Oct-April	x		x		x	
Spy	Bright red, some green or yellow spots	Fragrant, slightly tart	N.E./Upper Midwest	Nov-Feb	x	x	x	x	x	
Stayman	Bright red	Rich, mildly tart, tangy	Appalachia	Oct-April	x	x	x	x	x	
Wealthy	Red and deep red	Fine texture, tart	North	Sept	x	x	x		x	x
Winesap	Deep red, yellow streaked	Juicy, flavorful, firm	N.W. Appalachia	Nov-Dec	x	x	x		x	
York	Lopsided, red and green	Mild, firm	Appalachia	Oct-Feb	x		x		x	x

* Availablity and season may be extended by 2-3 months depending on storage

Salads

Apple-Cranberry Salad

Colorful and tasty for holiday meals. This is an old, special recipe of my mother's.

    1   quart ground cranberries
    ¾   cup sugar
    3   small packages lemon Jello®
    3   cups boiling water
    1   Tablespoons lemon juice
    1   teaspoon salt
    2   oranges (ground)
    4   medium Jonathan or Red Delicious apples
         (chopped)
    ½   cup diced celery
    ¼   cup chopped walnuts

   Mix cranberries with sugar, and let stand for 10 minutes. Mix Jello with boiling water. Add lemon juice and salt. Combine all fruit, celery and nuts into Jello. Pour into favorite 6 cup mold and place in refrigerator to set. Serves 12.
Riverland Ranch, Joyce Carver, Corvallis, OR

Blue Moon Salad

8 Haralson or McIntosh apples, unpeeled
2 Tablespoons lemon juice
½ cup Miracle Whip® (or other salad dressing)
¼ cup milk (or light cream)
1 cup celery (diced)
2 cups cooked ham (cut in cubes)
½ cup (2-ounces) blue cheese (crumbled)

Core apples and cut into bite-sized pieces. Toss in lemon juice to prevent browning and preserve flavor. Blend Miracle Whip and milk in bowl. Toss apples, celery and ham in bowl with dressing. Sprinkle with blue cheese. Garnish with star of apple wedges. Serves 8.
Hay Creek Apple Farm, Susan Fischer, Red Wing, MN

Make Ahead Party Apple Salad

Dressing
¼ cup sugar
2 Tablespoons flour
1 cup water
2 Tablespoons vinegar
1 teaspoon vanilla
1 Tablespoon butter

Mix all ingredients in a saucepan. Bring to a boil, stirring constantly. Remove from heat and cool.

Salad
3 red apples, diced but not peeled
1 cup minature marshmallows
½ cup chopped celery
½ cup chopped nuts
½ cups drained crushed pineapple
½ cup raisins

When dressing is cool, pour over the fruit mixture and toss lightly. Refrigerate overnight. Will keep for several days if stored in covered containers.
Jones Farm, Cornwall, NY

Apple-Red Cabbage Salad

    1   Medium head red cabbage, shredded
    2   Red Delicious apples, cored and thinly sliced
    1   medium onion, thinly sliced
    ⅓   cup vegetable oil
    ½   cup cider vinegar
    2   Tablespoons sugar
  1½   Tablespoons celery seed
    1   teaspoon salt
    ⅛   teaspoon pepper
    1   cup sour cream

Toss cabbage, apples and onions. Combine oil, vinegar, spices and sour cream. Pour over salad; toss to coat well.
Evie Ostendorf, Cedar Falls, IA

Incredapple Salad

Salad
    1   quart salad greens
    1   medium Golden Delicious apple, cored & chopped
    1   cup cheddar cheese cubes
    ½   cup chopped celery
    ½   cup golden raisins

Curry Dressing
    ⅔   cup vegetable oil
    ⅓   cup wine vinegar
    3   Tablespoons frozen concentrated apple juice,
         thawed and undiluted
    1   Tablespoons sugar
    ½   teaspoon celery salt
    ½   teaspoon curry powder

Measure all dressing ingredients into shaker jar; mix well. Makes 1 one-quarter cup dressing. Place all salad ingredients in bowl. Add curry dressing to taste and toss lightly. Serves 4
Stonegate Orchard, Dolores Christiansen, Slayton, MN

Apple-Celery-Kraut Salad

1 pound can sauerkraut
2 ribs celery
1 large apple (Golden Delicious, Cortland or Jonathan)
2 Tablespoons green onion
¼ cup white wine or 1 Tablespoon lemon juice
1 Tablespoon chives or 2 Tablespoons green onion
½ teaspoons each of celery seed, salt & sugar to taste

Rinse sauerkraut with cold water; drain. Slice celery thinly; core apple, cut into eights, and slice thinly crosswise. Chop green onion finely; snip chives (finely). Combine all ingredients and toss well.

Take care to cover apples well with sauerkraut to avoid discoloration. Chill several hours or overnight. Serves 4-6.

Shor-Lans U-Pick & Fruit Stand, Amy K. Gregory, Westfield, NY

Frozen Waldorf Salad

1 can (4 ounces) crushed pineapple
  water
3 eggs (beaten)
¾ cup sugar
¼ teaspoon salt
⅓ cup lemon juice
2 bananas or 1 cup finely chopped celery
3 medium Golden Delicious apples, diced
¾ cup chopped walnuts
  Tokay grapes as desired
1½ cups whipped cream

Drain pineapple, reserve juice, adding water to make ¾ cup. Combine juice with eggs, sugar, salt, lemon juice. Cook until thick. Cool, then add fruit, walnuts and whipped cream. Freeze in mold or 9"x9" pan. Makes 12 servings.

Editor's Note

The original recipe called for celery, but Carol's family prefers bananas. Both are delicious. This is very rich and can be served as dessert.

Faeth Orchards, Carol Faeth, Fort Madison, IA

Apple Cider Salad

1   6-ounce package orange flavored gelatin
4   cups apple cider
1   cup raisins
1   cup coarsely chopped apples
1   cup chopped celery
     juice and grated rind of 1 lemon
     lettuce

Dissolve gelatin in 2 cups hot apple cider, stir in raisins. Let cool. Add remaining 2 cups cider, chill until consistency of unbeaten egg white. Stir in apples, celery, lemon juice and rind. Pour into lightly oiled 6 cup mold. Chill until set. Unmold onto lettuce leaves. Makes 8 to 10 servings.
Miles Orchard, Marge Miles, Beaver Dam, KY

Yummy Apple Salad

2   cups diced apples, Red or Golden Delicious
4   teaspoons lemon juice
12   large marshmallows
⅔   cup chopped pecans or walnuts
¼   teaspoon salt
2   Tablespoons powdered sugar
⅓   cup commercial sour cream
⅔   cup mayonnaise
     lettuce leaf for serving

Core apples, leave red-skinned apples unpeeled. Dice them and sprinkle with lemon juice. Cut each large marshmallow into 4 pieces. Combine apples, nuts, marshmallows. Combine salt, powdered sugar, sour cream and mayonnaise.

Add mixture to apple mixture, tossing lightly with fork until apples are well coated. Arrange individual salads on a lettuce leaf. This recipe can be made ahead of time and refrigerated.
McGee's Apple Orchard, Mrs. Jim C. McGee, Columbus, KS

Layered Festive Apple-Pear Salad

6	ounces red gelatin (cherry, raspberry, or strawberry)
4	Red Delicious or Cortland apples
2	packets Knox Gelatin®
2	cups apple juice
8	ounce package cream cheese
2	cups walnuts, chopped
6	ounces lime gelatin
1	(20 ounce) can sliced pears, drained (reserve liquid)
½	cup chopped celery
	lettuce for salad plates
	garnish: 1 red apple, sliced, dipped in lemon juice
	1 avacado, peeled and sliced, dipped in lemon juice

Dissolve red gelatin in 1 cup boiling water. Add 1 cup cold water. Allow to thicken slightly; add 4 grated apples (core but do not remove peel). Chill until well thickened in a 9"x13"x2" pan (preferably glass). Prepare Knox Gelatin according to package instructions using 1 cup boiling apple juice, then adding 1 cup cold apple juice. Blend in cream cheese and walnuts.

Pour over red layer. Chill until thickened. Dissolve lime gelatin in one cup boiling water; add 1 cup of liquid from canned pears (add water if necessary to make one cup). Let thicken slightly, add sliced pears (cut up smaller if you wish), and chopped celery. Pour over white layer. Let set completely before serving.

To serve: cut into squares and place on lettuce leaves on chilled salad plates. Garnish top of each with a couple of unpeeled thin apple wedges and avocado slices.

Optional: for a festive Christmas salad, add a few drops mint flavoring (to taste) to white layer. Makes 12 3" squares.
Chuck Kinsey Family Farm, Shelia Marie Kinsey, Atlanta, MI

Main Dishes

Roast Duckling with Apple-Sesame Stuffing

2	ducklings (about 5 pounds)
2	packages stuffing mix
½	cup diced celery
¼	cup dried parsley flakes
4	tart apples, chopped
1½	teaspoons salt
2	teaspoons poultry seasoning
¼	teaspoon coarse black pepper
½	cup toasted sesame seeds
½	cup giblet stock
1	Tablespoon instant minced onion

Wash duckling inside and out, pat dry. Cook giblets to make stock. Prepare stuffing mix as directed on package. Add next 7 ingredients, mix thoroughly. Pour hot stock on onions, let stand 5 minutes. Add to stuffing and mix thoroughly. If stuffing is not moist enough, add a little more stock to taste.

Stuff ducklings, place on rack in large open roasting pan. Do not add water. Do not cover. Roast in moderate oven, 350° about 2½ hours, or until thoroughly done, 25 to 30 minutes per pound. Serves 8.

Note: To toast sesame seeds: spread in shallow pan, toast at 350°, 20-25 minutes, stirring occasionally.

Cox Orchard, Nancy Cox, Cleveland, MN

Yankee Stir-Fry

2-3   stalks celery
  1   sweet onion (bermuda type)
3-4   Tablespoons butter
  1   pound bay scallops or quartered sea scallops
  2   Tablespoons dry white wine
  2   Winesap or Rome Beauty apples, peeled and
       cut into chunks
  1   lemon
       salt, pepper and herbs* to taste

Slice celery on diagonal; cut onion into eight sections. Heat butter in heavy skillet or wok and stir fry celery and onion 2 or 3 minutes. Add scallops and wine (or 2 Tablespoons lemon juice). Stir; add apples and stir constantly 2-5 minutes (add more butter as needed) until scallops are cooked. Season to taste. Sprinkle with juice of half a lemon. Serve immediately. Very good with rice pilaf. Serves 4.

*Marilyn suggests McCormick's Fine Herbs,® but parsley and a bit of thyme would be good too. Be gentle with the seasonings.
Trout Brook Farm, Marilyn W. Benton, Madison, NJ

Jonathan Hamwich

12   slices rye bread
      mayonnaise
      mustard
12   slices baked ham
  6   Jonathan or Winesap apples, thinly sliced
12   slices Swiss cheese

Spread bread with equal amounts of mayonnaise and mustard. Layer each piece of bread with 1 slice of ham, 4 slices of apple and 1 slice of cheese. Place on cookie sheet and broil until cheese melts, and is lightly browned. Serve hot. Makes 12.
Twin Brook Farm, Faye Roth, Stronghurst, IL

Golden Delicious Apple Stew

1   pound lean beef or chucksteak, cubed
1   Tablespoon oil
3   cups apple juice
1   teaspoon salt
¼   teaspoons pepper
¼   teaspoon caraway seeds
1   bay leaf
8   small boiling onions
8   small carrots
2   Golden Delicious apples cored and diced
2   Tablespoons flour
2   Tablespoons cold water

Brown beef in oil. Stir in apple juice and seasonings. Cover and simmer 45 minutes or until tender. Stir in onions and carrots. Cover and simmer 30 minutes. Add apples during last 5 minutes. Blend flour and water together, stir into pan juices. Cook and stir until thickened. Garnish with parsley. Serves 4.

Marshall Apple Farm, Pat Marshall, Sebastopol, CA

Apple Sausage Casserole

6   bacon strips
8-10 links of brown-and-serve sausage
1   small onion chopped
3   cups chopped tart apples
½   cup chopped green pepper (optional)
⅔   cup diced celery
2   cups cooked rice
½   cup thinly sliced tart apples
3   Tablespoons brown sugar
½   cup apple juice

Fry bacon until crisp; remove bacon, drain on absorbent paper, crumble and set aside. Cut each sausage link into thirds; combine with onion, chopped apple, green pepper, celery, and cook in bacon drippings over low heat, 10 minutes.

Spread ⅔ cup of cooked rice on bottom of greased 1½ quart casserole; cover with half of sausage mixture, sprinkle with another ⅔ cup rice, remaining sausage mixture and lastly the remaining rice. Top with sliced apples. Sprinkle with crumbled bacon and brown sugar. Pour apple juice over all. Cover casserole. Bake at 350° for about 45 minutes. Serves 6 to 8.

Josephine Betzold, Bayfield, WI

Apple Cider Glazed Ham

        4-5   pounds ham
        2   cups fresh apple cider
        2   cinnamon sticks
        ½   teaspoon (16) whole cloves
        ½   teaspoon (16) whole allspice
        ¼   cup honey
        4   teaspoons cornstarch
                Thin sliced red and green apples (Haralson &
                Greening or any red and green varieties)

Bake ham as directed. Combine cider and spices in a saucepan; bring to a boil. Reduce heat; simmer 15 minutes. Remove spices. Mix honey and cornstarch; stir into cider. Cook over medium heat until thick, stirring constantly. Begin glazing 30 minutes before ham is done. Fifteen minutes later, remove ham from oven, arrange apple slices on top. Continue to bake and glaze the ham until done. Serves 6.

Apple Ridge Orchard, Ann Steffen, Mazeppa, MN

Apple Cheddar Quiche

        1   Tablespoon chopped onion
        6   Tablespoons butter
        1¼   cups crushed stone-ground whole wheat crackers
        ¼   cup finely chopped walnuts
        2   large tart apples, peeled, cored, and sliced (2 cups)
        3   eggs
        1   cup cream style cottage cheese
        1   cup shredded cheddar cheese
        ¼   cup milk
        ½   teaspoon salt
                pepper
                ground nutmeg

Cook onion in butter until tender. Stir in crushed crackers and nuts. Press mixture into a 9 inch pie plate, forming a crust. Bake in 350° oven for 8 minutes. Meanwhile simmer apples in a small amount of water 3 to 5 minutes or until tender. Drain; arrange apples in crust.

In blender container or food processor bowl blend the eggs, cheeses, milk, salt and dash pepper until smooth. Pour into crust. Sprinkle nutmeg on top. Bake in a 325° oven about 45 minutes or until knife inserted off-center comes out clean. Let stand 10 minutes before serving. Serves 4-6.

Stonegate Orchard, Dolores Christiansen, Slayton, MN

Pork Chops in Creamy Apple Sauce

       4   medium pork chops
       1   cup chopped onion
       ½   cup water
       2   cups applesauce
       1   Tablespoon lemon juice
       ½   teaspoon pepper
       ½   cup sour cream

Brown chops in large frying pan. Remove and trim any excess fat from chops. Saute onions in frying pan. Add water to pan and deglaze. Reduce heat, add applesauce, lemon juice, and pepper. Mix well. Return chops to pan and smother with sauce. Cover and cook gently until chops are done through, about 30-40 minutes.

Remove chops to a warm platter. Add sour cream to applesauce mixture and heat, but do not boil. Pour over chops and serve. Serves 4.

Sunnyview Orchards, Francis & Stella Otto, East Jordan, MI

Apple Stuffed Pork Chops

This is equally easy to prepare in a conventional or microwave oven.

       8   ½ inch thick pork chops
       1   large onion, chopped
       2   Tablespoons margarine
       2   cups chopped apples, Jonathan or McIntosh
       ⅓   cup raisins, chopped
       1   teaspoon salt
       ¼   teaspoon pepper
       2   cups seasoned croutons
           rubbed sage to taste, about ¼ teaspoon

Sear pork chops, set aside. Saute onion in margarine. Stir in chopped apple, raisins, salt and pepper. Cook until warm. Stir in croutons and sage. Arrange 4 pork chops in oven-proof pan. Place half the stuffing on top of chops. Cover with remaining 4 chops. Top with remaining stuffing. Bake covered at 350° for about 1 hour.

Microwave: assemble in 8" round pan as directed above. Cover with plastic wrap. Cook on Medium High (70°) 14-18 minutes. Let stand 5 minutes. Serves 4.

Sunnyview Orchards, Francis & Stella Otto, East Jordan, MI

Ground Beef Apple Roll-Up

1	cup Jonathan or Spy apples, cored and chopped fine
1	cup shredded carrots
½	cup raisins
¼	cup water
1	teaspoon salt
2	pounds lean ground beef
1	cup bread crumbs
2	eggs
½	cup water
½	teaspoon dry mustard
⅛	teaspoon thyme
1	teaspoon basil
1	Tablespoon celery flakes
1	teaspoon salt
¼	teaspoon pepper
1	can beef boullion
1	can water
1	package noodles
6	Tablespoons butter
¼	cup sour cream (optional)
2	Tablespoons pickle relish (optional)

Combine apples, carrots, raisins, ¼ cup water and 1 teaspoon salt in small fry pan. Bring to boil. Simmer 3 minutes. Set aside.

Combine meat, crumbs, eggs, water, and seasonings in large bowl. Mix well with hands. On a long piece of waxed paper, pat out meat mixture flat to a 11"x15" rectangle. Spread apple mixture evenly over the meat. Starting at the narrow end of meat, roll up, jelly-roll fashion. Seals edges. Place seam side down in a 9"x13" aluminum baking dish. Pour can of beef boullion and a can of water over the meat roll. Bake 1 hour at 350°, basting occasionally with the broth in dish.

About 10 minutes before meat is done, cook noodles in a large saucepan until tender. Drain well. Toss with butter and keep warm. When meat is done, place on a large platter. Arrange noodles around the meat roll. Cover and return to oven to keep warm.

Skim grease from broth remaining in the meat pan. Add water to make 2 cups liquid if necessary. Thicken gravy. Remove from heat. If desired, add sour cream and relish, stirring in rapidly with wire whisk. Pour thickened sauce over meat and noodles. Serve at once. Makes 8 servings.

Schemenauer Orchards, Evelyn Schemenauer, Bangor, MI

Apple Harvest Chicken Roast

When the apples are all harvested, and the cider made, we celebrate with this meal.

Stuffing

2	cups diced apples (Spy or other tart baking apple)
½	cup finely chopped celery
2	Tablespoons butter
3	cups unseasoned croutons
¼	teaspoon cinnamon
¼	teaspoon ginger
½	teaspoon rubbed sage
1	Tablespoon dried parsley
1	beaten egg
½	teaspoon salt
1	Tablespoon maple syrup
½	cup cider
4-5	pounds roasting chicken

Sauerkraut

3	cups thinly sliced onions
3	Tablespoons butter
1	cup cider
¼	teaspoon cumin
1	quart sauerkraut

Stuffed Apples

8	Northern Spy apples
8	Tablespoons each of raisins and brown sugar
½	stick butter
	cinnamon for dusting top of apples
¼	cup butter, melted
	paprika, enough to sprinkle on chicken
	maple syrup for basting
	approximately 1 cup cider to prevent sauerkraut from scorching

Saute apples and celery in butter for 5 minutes. Toss with rest of stuffing ingredients. Lightly stuff chicken; truss.

Cook onions in butter 2 minutes. Mix with cider, cumin and sauerkraut; put into large roasting pan. Place chicken, breast side down, on sauerkraut. Roast at 375°, allowing 25 minutes per pound. After 30 minutes, turn chicken breast side up.

continued on next page

Core (not all way through) 8 apples. Peel upper third of each apple. Stuff with raisins and brown sugar and small pat of butter. Sprinkle apples with cinnamon. Place apples around chicken. Baste chicken with ¼ cup melted butter. Sprinkle paprika on chicken. Roast for an hour, or until chicken is done. Check occasionally to see that sauerkraut-onion mixture does not scorch. Add more cider if necessary.

During final 15 minutes, baste chicken and apples with maple syrup 2-3 times. When roast is done and apples are fork tender, remove chicken and apples to a plate temporarily. Spoon sauerkraut mixture onto a large platter. Place chicken on the center of sauerkraut, remove trussing string. Position apples around chicken. Serves 6-8.

Chuck Kinsey Family Farm, Shelia Marie Kinsey, Atlanta, MI

Flanders Pork and Apples

2	pounds pork shoulder or loin sliced ½ inch thick
12	small white onions
2	Tablespoons flour
½	cup dry white wine
½	cup chicken broth or condensed consomme
	salt and pepper to taste
1	teaspoon dried oregano and rosemary mixed or 1 Tablespoon fresh, chopped
1	teaspoon minced parsley
1	pound tart cooking apples (Rome or Cortland)

Trim fat off pork slices and fry out in heavy skillet. Skim out the brown particles; saute pork and onions in fat. Remove to a medium casserole. Pour off all but 2 Tablespoons of fat. Stir in flour and slowly add wine and broth, stirring until sauce is smooth and thick.

Season sauce to taste with salt and pepper, add herbs, and pour over casserole mixture. Cover tightly and bake 2 hours in a 300° oven. (If your casserole lid does not fit tightly, cover the casserole first with aluminum foil, and then put the lid on.) When casserole has baked 1½ hours, stir in peeled and quartered apples, cover again, and finish baking.

Serve with mashed sweet potatoes, and buttered green beans, and cranberry relish. Serves 6.

Scholl and Sons Orchards, Irma Scholl, Richland Center, WI

Applesauce Meatloaf

¼ cup plus 2 Tablespoons applesauce
½ cup bread crumbs
1 teaspoon salt
½ teaspoon Worchestershire sauce
1 teaspoon prepared mustard
½ cup finely chopped onion
¼ cup finely chopped green pepper
1 pound lean ground beef
1 egg, slightly beaten
½ cup milk

½ teaspoon prepared mustard
3 teaspoons brown sugar
¼ cup catsup

Combine first 10 ingredients. Form into a loaf in baking dish. Mix remaining ingredients, pour on top of loaf. Bake uncovered at 350° degrees for 1 hour. Serves 3-4.

Variation: Shape meatloaf into a round (8") pie plate. Make a depression in the top with a spoon or bowl. Mix and pour into the depression:

½ cup applesauce
1 Tablespoon brown sugar
1 Tablespoon vinegar
1 teaspoon prepared mustard

Bake as directed above, or 20 minutes on High in microwave. Turn once during cooking.
McGee's Apple Orchard, Mrs. Jim C. McGee, Columbus, KS

Pork Pot-au-Feu

Pork, sweet potatoes and apples are natural companions. Serve this soup-stew with plenty of crusty bread and butter for a hearty one-dish meal.

2	pounds lean pork (cut for stew)
	garlic salt, pepper, dry mustard
2	cans consomme diluted with 2 cans water
1	medium onion, grated or 1 Tablespoon instant minced onion
1	medium cabbatge (2-3 pounds) shredded coarsely
¼	cup ketchup
1	cup dried pinto or light kidney beans, soaked overnight
1	quart boiling water
2	medium sweet potatoes, cubed
2	medium white potatoes, cubed
2	York apples, cored and cubed*
2	teaspoons salt
1	teaspoon allspice
½	cup dry sherry or dry red wine

Sprinkle pork chunks with garlic salt, pepper and a little dry mustard. Set aside. Bring diluted consomme, onion and one-third of cabbage to a boil. Add the seasoned pork; bring to a boil. Cover and boil gently for 1 hour.

Add ketchup, beans, another third of cabbage and 1 quart boiling water. Cover and boil gently for another hour. Skim off any excess fat.

Add the last third of cabbage, potatoes and apples, 2 teaspoon salt, allspice and sherry or wine. Boil 45 minutes to 1 hour or until potatoes are tender. Serves 6-8.

*Can substitute Golden Delicious or Stayman, but peel first.
Mountain Green Farm, Sally L. Sharp, Washington, VA

Side Dishes & Miscellaneous

Apple Fritters

> 1   egg, beaten
> ⅓   cup milk
>   oil for frying
> 1   cup flour
> ¼   teaspoon salt
> 1½   teaspoons baking powder
> 2   Golden Delicious apples, diced
>   powdered sugar

In a heavy pot, begin heating cooking oil to 365° for deep frying.

Beat egg and milk into dry ingredients. Stir in apples. Drop dough, one tablespoon at a time, into the hot oil. Fry until golden brown, approximately 5 minutes. Drain fritters on paper towels for 3 to 5 minutes. Roll in powdered sugar. Makes 12 to 15 fritters.

Longhi's Orchard, JoAnn Longhi, Collinsville, IL

Variation
Beth Bush of Bush Orchards, St. Joseph, MO uses Jonathans, cored and peeled, but she slices them ⅛" thick, dips them into the batter, and then fries them in butter. Beth serves them with syrup for breakfast.

Apple-Sausage Stuffed Acorn Squash

    3   acorn squash
    1   pound ground sausage
    2   large unpeeled Spy apples
    ⅓   cup packed, either brown sugar, maple sugar
        molasses, maple syrup or honey
    ½   teaspoon cinnamon
    ¼   teaspoon nutmeg
    ⅛   teaspoon cloves
    ⅛   teaspoon ginger
    ⅓   cup dried currants or raisins
    ⅓   cup butter
    ½   cup chopped nuts (optional)

Cut squash lengthwise into halves; remove seeds. Place cut-side down in baking pans with hot water about ½" deep. Cover and bake 20 minutes in medium hot (375°) oven. Meanwhile saute sausage until pink color changes to beige. Do not overcook.

Add finely chopped apples to sausage for last few minutes. Drain off grease. Mix together brown sugar (or your choice, or any combination to equal ⅓ cup), cinnamon, nutmeg, cloves, ginger. Sprinkle over sausage and apples; mix well. Stir in currants or raisins and nuts. Remove squash from oven. Place cut side up in pans. Divide sausage mixture between halves. Put some butter on top of mixture. Cover pans. Return to oven and bake at 375° for about 30 minutes.

Squash should be cooked until easily pierced with a fork. Time depends on squash maturity. Serve for breakfast or as a side dish with pork roast. Serves 6.

Doc Carey Homestead Orchards, Onalee Carey, Atlanta, MI

Variations
1. Evie Ostendorf of Cedar Falls, IA bakes squash halves; salts and peppers them then stuffs with mixture of 2 peeled, cored and diced Cortland apples mixed with 2 Tablespoons softened butter, ¼ cup honey, ¼ cup raisins. Return to oven 20 minutes or until tender.
2. Helen Lamb of Peaches 'n' Cream Farm, Seymour, MO uses 2 pounds butternut squash, cut and pared. She puts them in an ungreased baking dish, and tops with 2 baking apples, cored and cut into ½" slices. Mix together ½ cup packed brown sugar, ¼ cup melted butter, 1 Tablespoon flour, 1 teaspoon salt and ½ teaspoon mace or cinnamon and sprinkle over top. Cover and bake at 350° for 50-60 minutes or until tender.
3. Jan Burnap of Burnap Fruit Farms in Sodos, NY sent a very similar recipe. She adds nutmeg to her topping.

Moist Apple-Sausage Stuffing

1   pound bread, sliced (about 24 slices), cubed
2-4 medium Golden Delicious apples
2   onions
4-8 large celery sticks and leaves
1   pound sausage
2   cubes chicken boullion, dissolved in 1 cup boiling water
1   teaspoon salt
½   teaspoon pepper

Fry sausage. Put in large bowl. Chop onions and celery sticks and leaves. Saute in pan. Add to sausage. Core and chop apples. Mix all ingredients in large bowl. Makes enough to stuff a 12-16 pound turkey. Any stuffing left over can be put in casserole and baked at 350° for 1½ hours or baked in microwave oven. Makes about 12 cups or will stuff a 12-16 pound turkey.
Dutch Acres, Joyce Kayim, Allegan, MI

Variation
Shirley Damm, Colonial Orchards, West Paris, ME, sent a very similar recipe, but she doesn't use sausage. Saute 1 cup each chopped onion and celery in ½ cup butter. Flavor with 1 teaspoon sage, ½ cup chopped walnuts. Use same amounts of everything else, except Shirley suggests using 6 cups soft breadcrumbs and ½ cup apple cider instead of chicken boullion. She also suggests glazing the turkey with ¼ cup apple cider, ¼ cup honey and ¼ cup melted butter.

Apple & Carrot Casserole

6   large carrots
5   large Red Delicious or York apples
5   Tablespoons sugar
5   Tablespoons flour
½   teaspoon nutmeg
     butter
½   cup orange juice

Slice carrots thinly and cook in salted water for 5 minutes; drain. Slice apples and cook in clear water 5 minutes; drain. Layer carrots and apples in casserole. Mix sugar, flour and nutmeg and sprinkle over top. Dot with butter. Pour orange juice over all. (Can be made ahead and baked just before serving.) Bake 30-40 minutes in 350° oven. Serves 6.
Gobbler's Knob Orchard, Rose Auker, McAlisterville, PA

Stuffed Cinnamon Apples

1½-2   cups water
½   cup sugar
½   cup cinnamon candies (red hots)
6   whole cloves
6   Winesap or Jonathan apples
1   cup cream cheese (softened)
⅓   cup mayonnaise
4   Tablespoons chopped nuts

Boil water, sugar, candies and cloves until candies are dissolved and syrup is red. Peel and core apples (leaving them whole). Cut away a hole about 1 inch in diameter through the core. Drop apples in syrup and boil slowly, carefully turning until apples are tender and well colored. Drain and chill. Mix cheese and mayonnaise. Stuff apples with cheese mixture; sprinkle chopped nuts on top of cheese. Serve on lettuce leaf.
Eckert Orchards, Inc., Judy Eckert, Millstadt, IL

Navy Bean Apple Casserole

2   cups dried navy beans
1½   teaspoon salt
⅓   cup brown sugar
3   large tart apples sliced (Spy or Jonathan)
¼   pound salt pork or ½ cup diced bacon

Wash beans and put in 3 quart saucepan; add cold water to come 2" above beans and soak overnight. Next morning drain, add 4 cups fresh water and salt. Bring to boil and simmer gently for 2 hours in covered dish; drain, saving water.

Arrange beans and apple slices in casserole in alternate layers. Pour in 2 cups liquid and lay pork on top. Bake covered in a very slow oven (250°) or crockpot for 1½ hours, or until beans are light brown and thoroughly cooked. If they become dry, add more of the cooking liquid, apple cider, or apple juice. Serves 5-7.
Alpine Orchards, Mrs. Janice L. Schweitzer, Comstock Park, MI

Apples 'n Sweet Potatoes

    5   *sweet potatoes*
    4   *large juicy apples, peeled, cored and sliced*
½-1 *cup brown sugar*
    2   *teaspoons salt*
  ¼   *cup butter*
    1   *teaspoon nutmeg*
  ¼   *cup hot water*
  ½   *cup honey*

Boil sweet potatoes in water until almost tender. Peel and slice when cooled. Alternate layers of sliced potatoes and apples beginning with sweet potatoes and ending with sliced apples. Cover each double layer with some of the sugar, salt and bits of butter. On top layer of apples sprinkle remaining brown sugar and dots of butter. Then sprinkle with nutmeg. Mix hot water and honey and pour evenly over top.

Bake in a 400° oven until apples are tender, approximately ½ to ¾ hour. Delicious with ham or turkey. Serves 8.

The Apple Place, Judy Taylor, Miramonte, CA

Variations

1. Evie Ostendorf, Cedar Falls IA: bakes her casserole topped with ½ cup chopped pecans.

2. Alice Adae, A&M Farm, Midland OH: Toss apples with brown sugar, chopped pecans and use cinnamon rather than nutmeg. Omit honey and water. Bake covered. Just before serving both Evie and Alice Sprinkle 1-2 cups miniature marshmallows over top and broil until lightly browned.

Baked Apple Surprises

    4   *Granny Smith or Greening apples*
  ⅓   *cup Grape-Nuts®*
  ⅓   *cup brown sugar*
  ½   *teaspoon cinnamon*
    2   *Tablespoons soft butter*
          pinch salt

Core apples and peel a bit off top. Grease bottom of a shallow pan, set apples in it. Combine remaining ingredients, fill apple cavities. Cover bottom of pan with water. Bake at 400°, 50-60 minutes or until done.

Evie Ostendorf, Cedar Falls, IA

Apples á la Creola

    1   cup sugar
    1   cup water
    6   large McIntosh or Cortland apples
    1   Tablespoon gelatin, soaked in ¼ cup cool water
    ¾   cup chopped nuts
    1   cup brown sugar
    ¼   cup cream or milk
    1   Tablespoon butter
    1   cup whipped cream

Boil granulated sugar and 1 cup water for 5 minutes. Peel and core apples, cut in half, cook in syrup until tender. Remove apples and place in serving dish. Add softened gelatin to syrup and stir until smooth, pour over apples, put on layer of nuts, keeping enough nuts out for topping.

Cook brown sugar and cream to soft ball stage, add butter and pour over apples and nuts. Set aside to cool. When ready to serve, cover with whipped cream and sprinkle with nuts. Serves 6.

Oxbow Orchards, Jean Rhinebolt, Oxbow, ME

Stewed Apples in White Wine

    6   Jonathan or Ida Red apples
    3   Tablespoons butter
    ½   cup white wine
    ½   cup water
    1   cup sugar
    2" cinnamon stick
    1   Tablespoon lemon juice
    1   Tablespoon grated lemon peel

Wash and core apples. Cut into thick slices. Saute in butter in deep fry pan, 5 minutes. Combine remaining ingredients in saucepan. Simmer 5 minutes. Pour over apples. Cook uncovered until apples are tender. Do not overcook apples. Serve warm. A nice accompaniment to gingerbread. Serves 6.

Schemenauer Orchards, Evelyn Schemenauer, Bangor, MI

Roman Peanut Crunch

>   4   *English muffins*
>   *chunky peanut butter*
>   2   *medium Rome Beauties or Winesaps*
>   12   *slices bacon*
>   *cinnamon*

Split and lightly toast English muffins. Spread with chunky peanut butter. Core the apples, and do not peel. Cut each apple in 4 slices. Cut each slice of bacon in half (24 pieces), partially cook, drain.

Put apple slice on top of peanut butter, sprinkle with cinnamon to taste. Put three bacon pieces on top. Broil until bacon is done. Serves 8.

Trout Brook Farm, Marilyn Benton, Chester, NJ

Variation

Nichols U-Pick Orchard, Rachel Nichols, Troutsville, VA spreads Golden Delicious apple slices with smooth peanut butter, and decorates with raisins—a thrill for children!

Broiled Apple Rings

>   5-6   *medium Red Delicious apples, cored and sliced into*
>   *30 rings ½" thick*
>   ¼   *teaspoon ground cinnamon*
>   ¼   *cup unsalted butter or margarine, melted*
>   2   *Tablespoons granulated sugar*

Arrange apple rings in a single layer on 2 or 3 lightly buttered, heavy baking sheets. Stir cinnamon onto butter and brush on apple rings. Sprinkle with sugar. Broil 4 to 6 inches from heat source, 8 to 10 minutes, until apples are tender and lightly browned.

Watch apples carefully to prevent burning. Turn sheets around once or twice if necessary to ensure even browning. As each batch of apples is done, cover loosely with alumninum foil and keep warm in a 200° oven if possible. Makes 30 rings.

Bush Orchards, Beth Bush, St. Joseph, MO

Appletizer

Cortland or Golden Delicious apples, unpeeled
lemon juice
¼ cup nuts
6 ounces cream cheese

Core apples and slice into ¼ inch rings. Dip into lemon juice, blotting off excess. Mix finely chopped nuts into cream cheese. Spread on half of the apple slices. Top with another slice of apple (sandwich style).
Shirley Buckholz, Beaver Falls, PA

Stuffed Celery

1 red apple, finely chopped
¼ cup walnuts, finely chopped
salad dressing and/or cream cheese
celery, washed and cut into 2" lengths
lemon juice (optional)

Combine apple, nuts and cream cheese and/or salad dressing in small bowl. Use to stuff celery. Sprinkle with lemon juice before serving.
Shirley Buckholz, Beaver Falls, PA

Apple Bites

Cut Red Delicious apples into chunks. Roll in mayonnaise, then roll in crisp chopped bacon, or chopped nuts, or grated cheese. Serve with a tooth pick.
Hazel Lacy, Campbellsville, KY

Spiced Lady Apples

4   quarts Lady apples (whole, unpeeled) about 4 pounds or 40 apples (alternate, very small Winesaps)
     whole cloves
1   pint vinegar
1   pint water
4   cups sugar
3   3" cinnamon sticks
2   Tablespoons whole allspice
½   teaspoon ground mace

After washing apples, prick each with fork and stick with 2 cloves. Combine vinegar, water, sugar and spices, bring to a boil and boil syrup about 10 minutes, until slightly thickened. Add apples. Simmer over low heat until tender—about 30 minutes. Let stand in a cool place overnight.

Next day remove spices and bring syrup to a boil. Pour over apples which have been packed into hot sterilized jars. Process in boiling water 20 minutes according to canner manufacturer's directions. Yields 4 quarts.

Serve with roasts, curry dishes or on a condiment tray.

Mountain Green Farm, Sally Sharp, Washington, VA

Quick Apple-Cranberry Relish

1   cup chopped apple (Jonathan or McIntosh)
1   cup whole raw cranberries
1   Tablespoon candied ginger, finely chopped
2   Tablespoons orange juice
     sugar to taste (about ⅔ cup)

Mix ingredients in small sauce pan and simmer slowly until most of the cranberries have burst and the apples are soft. Serve warm or cold. Makes ¾ cup.

Sunnyview Orchards, Stella & Francis Otto, East Jordan, MI

Quick Apple Stick Relish

3 unpared apples, cored and cut in small strips (3 cups)
⅔ cup chopped onion
½ cup chopped dill pickle
½ cup sugar
¼ cup vinegar

Mix apples, onions, and pickle. Combine sugar and vinegar; toss with apple mixture. Chill. Serve as meat accompaniment. Makes 6 servings.
Bippert's Farms, Eileen Bippert, Elma, NY

Musselli Cereal

1 banana, diced
3 Golden Delicious, or Winesap apples, shredded, unpeeled
¼ cup nuts, chopped
½ cup dates, chopped
1 teaspoon vanilla
1 teaspoon salt
1 cup pineapple, chopped
1½ cups quick oats
1¼ cups water

Mix banana, apples, nuts and dates together. Add vanilla, salt, pineapple, oats, and then pour water over top of it and let stand overnight in refrigerator. Makes a good breakfast. If you prefer you can use apple juice instead of water. Serves 8.
Academy Gardens, Inc., Wilma Jean Thiry, Elburn, IL

Apple Soup

        4½ cups boiling water
         3 Tablespoons quick tapioca
        4½ cups applesauce
         2 teaspoons cinnamon
         1 teaspoon salt
        ½   cup sugar

Stir the tapioca into boiling water. Cook until clear. Add applesauce, cinnamon, salt and sugar. Simmer 10 minutes. Serve hot, or chill thoroughly and serve cold. Garnish with lemon or cinnamon.

Day Orchard, Mrs. Glenn Day, Mondamin, IA

Apple Cider Jelly

         5 8-ounce jelly glasses
            paraffin
         4 cups fresh apple cider
         1 1¾-ounce package fruit pectin
         5 cups sugar
            red food color (optional)

Prepare glasses and lids and melt parafin. In large saucepan or dutch oven mix apple cider and fruit pectin well. Heat mixture, over high heat, stirring constantly until rapidly boiling. Stir in sugar, boil again 1 minute stirring constantly.

Remove from heat, stir in red food coloring (few drops) if desired. With metal spoon skim off foam. Fill scalded glasses to within ½ inch of top. Pour on melted wax. Let stand until paraffin hardens and jelly cools.

Apple Ridge Orchard, Ann Steffen, Mazeppa, MN

"I make my own apple jelly by using cider. I follow the same recipe for jelly in the Sure-Jell® box, but instead of boiling the apples to get the juice out, just heat the cider and you save a lot of time."

Editor

Scalloped Apples

4-6	large apples, peeled, cored and sliced (Mutsu, Stayman, or Golden Delicious)
½	cup water
2	Tablespoons granulated sugar
2	Tablespoons brown sugar
1	teaspoon cinnamon
¼	teaspoon allspice
1½	teaspoons lemon juice
1	Tablespoon fine bread crumbs
	nutmeg
1	Tablespoon butter or margarine

Preheat oven to 400°. Put apples in a buttered shallow baking dish 8"x8". Add water. Mix sugars, cinnamon and allspice. Sprinkle over apples along with lemon juice, breadcrumbs and nutmeg. Dot with butter.

Bake about 45 minutes until apples are soft. While still hot, spoon any excess liquid in the pan over apples and gently pat down top layer of fruit until it is moist.

Serve warm or cold as a side dish or as a dessert with a dollop of sour cream or yogurt. Serves 4-6.

Mountain Green Farm, Sally Sharp, Washington, VA.

Apple Muffins

2	cups sugar
3	eggs
3	cups flour
1	teaspoon salt
1	teaspoon cinnamon
1	teaspoon baking powder
1	teaspoon soda
1	cup salad oil
3	cups grated Cortland or Golden Delicious apples
2	teaspoons vanilla
¾	cup walnuts
¾	cup raisins or dates

Combine all ingredients in large bowl. Pour into lightly greased muffin tins. Bake at 350°. A half walnut on top is good. Serve hot. Makes 3 dozen.

Note: To those who can't use 3 dozen muffins at once: Increase baking powder to 3 teaspoons and store unused batter tightly covered in refrigerator. Use within 5 days.

Carrie's Apple Stand, Mrs. John M. Phillips, Red Creek, NY

TuttiFrutti Scones

½   cup cider
½   cup seedless raisins
⅔   cup chopped dried fruit (apples, apricots, peaches, etc.)
⅔   cup chopped glace fruit or dates
2   cups flour
2   teaspoons baking powder
    pinch of salt
1½   Tablespoons butter
6   Tablespoons milk

Put cider, dried fruit, raisins, and glace fruit into a saucepan. Bring to a boil and boil steadily until most of the cider is evaporated. Allow to become cold. Sift flour, baking powder, and salt in bowl. Cut in butter until mixture resembles fine breadcrumbs. Stir in fruit and cider and enough milk to mix to a firm consistency. (Enough milk worked in so that you can pick up all the flour).

Get out pastry cloth. Flour it. Put dough on cloth and knead several times. Roll out or press down to ½ inch thickness. Using a 2 inch plain cutter, stamp out 12 scones. (I just cut the dough in squares· Scones in England are usually just cut.)

Bake on a lightly floured baking tray. (This is just flour. Do not grease). Bake at 425° for 10 to 15 minutes. Serve warm with butter and jam. They are good cold too. Serve with hot tea with a spot of milk in it.

Cricket Hill Orchards, Inc., Anna Outman, Pocahontas, IL

Apple Bread I

⅓   cup shortening
1   cup sugar
1   egg
2   cups flour
¾   teaspoon baking powder
½   teaspoon baking soda
⅓   cup orange juice
1   cup diced apples, (Ida Red, Cortland or Mutsu)

Mix shortening, sugar and egg. Add rest of ingredients and orange juice (dilute—not concentrate). Bake in greased pans at 350° for 50-60 minutes. Makes 2-3 loaves.

Smith Bros. Farms, Inc., Alan Smith, North Rose, NY

Apple Bread II

¼ cup shortening
⅔ cup sugar
2 eggs, beaten
2 cups sifted flour
1 teaspoon baking powder
1 teaspoon baking soda
1 teaspoon salt
2 cups coarsely grated, peeled McIntosh or Wealthy
   apples
1 Tablespoon grated lemon rind
⅔ cup chopped walnuts

Cream shortening and sugar until light and fluffy, beat in eggs. Sift next 4 ingredients and add alternately to egg mixture with apple. Stir in lemon rind and nuts.

Bake in greased and floured loaf pan, 9"x5"x3" in preheated 350° oven for 1 hour. Cool before slicing. Makes 1 loaf.

John McIlquham Orchards, Mrs. John McIlquham, Chippewa Falls, WI

Ruth's Applesauce

Apples, favorite variety
sugar to taste
cinnamon to taste
juice of fresh lemon (or lemons)

Wash and slice apples into eighths, (do not peel). Cut away core. Cut each eighth into 2 or 3 parts. Place in large cooking vessel (may have to use 2 or 3 pots). Add about 2 or 3 cups of water (depending upon size of pot).

Cook stirring frequently to prevent apples from sticking to bottom of pot (add water if necessary). When all are soft place small amounts in Foley Food Mill, and grind until most of the apples have gone through the sieve. The skin of the apple adds character to the sauce when riced through the food mill.

After apples are sieved, add sugar, cinnamon and lemon juice, small amounts at a time, to taste. The sauce may be canned in the usual manner or frozen in freezer bags, jars or freezer containers.

Variation: Plums (Italian small purple variety) are a great addition to the sauce. Cook together with the apples and omit the cinnamon.

Ruth Cates, Silver Spring, MD

Beverages

Apple Wassail

1	gallon sweet cider
3	teaspoons ground allspice
1	teaspoons ground cloves
½	teaspoon ground nutmeg
4	sticks cinnamon
	juice of 8 oranges
	juice of 4 lemons
2	cups sugar

Simmer all together for ½ hour. Can be stored in refrigerator and heated as wanted. Serve hot.

Variations
1. Joyce Parker, Apple Spot Orchard, Sibley, MO sent a similar recipe, which she sweetens with ¼ cup brown sugar. Instead of the fruit juices, Joyce adds 1 Tablespoon dried orange peel. She uses whole spices, and removes them before serving.
2. Mrs. Jim McGee of McGee's Apple Orchard in Columbus, KS adds juice of only one lemon and 2 oranges, and sweetens with ¼ cup honey. Mrs. McGee warns. "DO NOT BOIL CIDER." Serve in mugs with cinnamon stick.

Party Perked Mulled Cider

      1   gallon farm cider
      3   2-inch cinnamon sticks
      5   whole allspice
     16   whole cloves
      1   whole nutmeg
      1   cup light brown sugar

Pour cider into large perculator (do not use a drip coffeemaker). Place spices and brown sugar into perculator basket and perk as you would coffee. Serve directly from perculator. Spices may be saved for another time.

Eckert Orchards, Judy Eckert, Millstadt, IL

Mulled Cider

      1   gallon fresh cider
      1   quart cranberry juice
      1   liter whiskey
      1   cinnamon stick
      6   allspice
     10   cloves stuck in an orange
     ¼   cup brown sugar

Mix all together. Float orange in liquid. Heat. Serve warm.

Burnap Fruit Farms, Jan Burnap, Sodus, NY

Hot Apple Cider Snap

This is like drinking warm apple pie.

      1   gallon fresh cider (without preservatives)
      3   ounces frozen orange juice concentrate
      1   cup sugar
      2   teaspoons cinnamon
      3   teaspoons allspice
     ½   teaspoon nutmeg

Begin heating cider in a pan. Add all ingredients and bring to a boil. Simmer a few minutes. Skim off excess seasonings. Serve hot.

Smith Bros. Farms, Inc., Alan Smith, North Rose, NY

Apple Sherbert Punch

  1   *quart orange sherbert or rainbow*
  4   *cups apple juice*
  4   *cups orange juice*
  1   *bottle (28-ounce) lemon lime soda pop*
      fresh mint sprigs (optional)

Pour juices over balls of sherbert in punchbowl. Add soda pop and garnish with mint.

Suggestion

Freeze small apples in apple juice and soda pop in half full quart milk carton; use in punch bowl to keep cold.

Alpine Orchards, Mrs. Janice L. Schweitzer, Comstock Park, MI

Cider Punch

   1   *gallon apple cider*
  12   *ounces frozen lemonade, undiluted*
4-5   *spiced apple rings*
   1   *lemon, sliced*

Stir together apple cider and thawed lemonade; mix well. Garnish by floating apple rings and lemon slices on punch. Serves 16 people.

Stony Creek Orchard, Carol Ross, Romeo, MI

Apple Refresher

A refreshingly light ice cream drink for any time of the year!

  1   *quart chilled apple cider or juice*
  1   *pint vanilla ice cream*
  ½   *teaspoon cinnamon (to suit your taste)*

Mix ingredients together in blender until frothy. Serve immediately. Serves 2-3.
Variation
1 cup apple juice, ½ cup grape juice, 2 Tablespoons yogurt, ¼ cup raisins. Blend until smooth and creamy.
Sunnyview Orchards, Francis & Stella Otto, East Jordan, MI

Spiced Tea

  1½   *quarts boiling water*
  1   *cup sugar*
  3   *cups apple juice*
  2   *cups pineapple juice*
  2   *lemons sliced*
  2   *oranges sliced*
      ground cloves to taste
      ground cinnamon to taste
  3   *tea bags*

Combine all ingredients in a large saucepan, simmer 15 minutes. Remove teabags and serve in mugs. Yields about 3 quarts. Save leftover tea in a glass jar with a lid. Heat up the tea when you just want 1 cup.
Hazel Lacy, Campbellsville, KY

Desserts

Best-Ever Caramel Apples

For best results use a candy thermometer.

10	Red Delicious or Jonathan apples
10	wooden skewers
2	cups granulated sugar
1	cup light corn syrup
1	cup heavy cream
1	cup evaporated milk
½	teaspoon salt
1	generous teaspoon vanilla
	Coarsely chopped pecans

Wash apples thoroughly and dry. Remove stems and insert sturdy wooden skewers. Set aside.

In saucepan, cook sugar, syrup and cream over medium heat, stirring constantly to 235°. Gradually add half of the evaporated milk. Allow caramel to heat up to 235° again, then add rest of evaporated milk. Continue cooking, stirring constantly to 242°.

Remove pan from heat; let stand undisturbed for 10 minutes. Stir in salt and vanilla. Set mixture over hot water.

Dip each apple, twirling to coat. Allow excess caramel to drip back into pan. Immediately roll bottom half of apple in chopped pecans. Place on well-buttered tray and allow to cool completely. These won't last long, but can be stored up to one week in fridge, covered with plastic wrap.

Martina Boudreau, Editor

Apple Dumplings

Your favorite sweet pie crust recipe (try the one in
this book with "Special Apple Pie", page 46)
6   medium Jonathan apples
    sugar
    cinnamon

Sauce

2   cups water
1   cup sugar
¼   stick butter
½   teaspoon cinnamon

Make the pie crust and roll out. Cut dough into squares large
enough to wrap around your apples. Peel and core apples. Place
each apple on a square of dough. Fill the hole with sugar and a
dash of cinnamon. Fold dough up over the apples and seal. Place
in baking dish.

Make sauce by bringing all sauce ingredients to boil in small
saucepan. Pour over apples in pan. Bake approximately one hour
at 350°. Serves 6.

Note: If you like a syrup rather than sauce, reduce water to 1 cup.

Day Orchard, Mrs. Glenn Day, Mondamin, IA

Apple Pie Filling

4½   cups sugar
1   cup cornstarch
2   teaspoons cinnamon
¼   teaspoon nutmeg
1   teaspoon salt
10   cups water
3   Tablespoons lemon juice
5½-6 pounds apples or 24 cups

In large pan blend first 4 ingredients. Add salt, stir in water.
Cook and stir until clear, thick and bubbling—sort of foamy. Add
raw apples to syrup as it is cooking and heat through. Add lemon
juice. Pack apples in jars leaving 1" head space, fill with hot syrup.
To seal process 15 minutes for pints and 20 minutes for quarts,
in water bath. Pressure cook 10 pounds for 10 minutes for quarts.

Miles-Barrett Orchard, Marge Miles, Beaver Dam, KY

Crow's Nest Pie

Crust and Topping

    1   carton (16 ounces) sour cream
    ½   cup flour (scant)
    1   teaspoon baking soda

Filling

    1   cup sugar
    2   Tablespoons flour
    ¼   teaspoon salt
    4   cups thinly sliced Spy or Cortland apples
    2   Tablespoons oleo or butter
    1   teaspoon cinnamon

Add flour to sour cream gradually. Add baking soda and mix well. Sift together sugar, flour, and salt for filling. Reserve a little to sprinkle over lower crust. Combine remainder with apples.

Pour ½ of sour cream batter into 10" pie plate. Push up around sides. Sprinkle with reserved sugar mixture. Add apple mixture; dot with butter. Sprinkle with cinnamon; cover with rest of sour cream batter. Bake 375° one hour. Top will be browned and crusty—serve warm. Pie will "set up" firmer as it cools. Serves 6-8.
Gehringer's Orchard and Cider Mill, Geri Gehringer, Bay City, MI

Shredded Apple Pie

Easy, no-fail apple pie. I use my cheese grater to shred the apples.

    1   unbaked deep dish pie shell
    1   cup sugar
    2   Tablespoons flour
    ½   teaspoon cinnamon
    5 or 6 large Golden Delicious or Stayman apples
    ½   stick melted margarine or butter
    1   beaten egg

Combine dry ingredients in large bowl. Fold in peeled and shredded apples. Mix melted butter with beaten egg and stir into apple mixture. Pour into pie shell. Bake 40-45 minutes at 350°. Serve warm with ice cream. DELICIOUS.
Nichols U-Pick Orchard, Rachel T. Nichols, Troutville, VA

Swedish Apple Pie

Very quick to prepare; the apples don't need to be peeled and there is no crust to be rolled out. A real hit with all who have tried it!

5-6   medium apples, Jonathan, Cortland, Golden
        Delicious or combination
  1   Tablespoon sugar
  1   Tablespoon cinnamon
  ¾   cup melted butter
  1   cup sugar
  1   cup flour
  1   egg
  ½   cup chopped nuts
      pinch of salt
      sprinkle of vanilla

Core and slice apples. Fill 9" or 10" pie plate ⅔ full with apples. Sprinkle with tablespoon each of sugar and cinnamon. Combine remaining ingredients. Pour over apples. Bake at 350° for 45 minutes. Serve hot or cold.

Sunnyview Orchards, Stella & Francis Otto, East Jordan, MI

Variation
Mrs. E. Wayne Anderson of Ottawa, KS makes a similar pie, which she says is more like a coffeecake. She uses 1½ cups of sugar, omits the butter and adds an extra egg. She chops her apples rather than slicing them and adds them to the batter prior to pouring it into the pie plate. Bake 35 minutes. Can be served for dessert with whipped cream or ice cream.

Special Apple Pie

Crust

1¾	cups all purpose flour
¼	cup sugar
1	teaspoon cinnamon
½	teaspoon salt
½	cup plus 2 Tablespoons butter (1¼ sticks)
¼	cup apple cider or water

Filling

8	McIntosh or Cortland apples, peeled, cored and sliced
1⅔	cups sour cream
1	cup sugar
⅓	cup all purpose flour
1	egg
2	teaspoons vanilla

Topping

1	cup chopped walnuts
½	cup all-purpose flour
⅓	cup firmly packed brown sugar
⅓	cup granulated sugar
1	Tablespoon cinnamon
	pinch salt
½	cup (1 stick) butter, room temperature

For Crust: Combine flour, sugar, cinnamon and salt in medium bowl. Cut in butter. Add apple cider (or water) and toss until evenly moistened. Gather into ball. Transfer to lightly floured board and roll into circle. Ease pastry into 11" pie tin (or deep 10") and flute a high edge. Set aside.

For Filling: Preheat oven to 450°. Combine apples, sour cream, sugar, flour, eggs and vanilla in large bowl and mix well. Spoon into crust. Bake 10 minutes. Reduce oven temperature to 350° and continue baking until filling is slightly puffed and golden brown, about 40 minutes. (If edges begin to brown too quickly, cover with strips of aluminum foil.)

For Topping: Meanwhile, combine walnuts, flour, sugars, cinnamon and salt in medium bowl and mix well. Blend in butter until mixture is crumbly. Spoon over pie and bake 15 minutes longer.

Barthel Fruit Farm, Mrs. Nora Barthel, Thiensville, WI

Walnut-Apple Pie

 1½ cups sugar
  3 Tablespoons flour
 1½ teaspoons ground cinnamon
  ¼ teaspoon ground nutmeg
  ¼ teaspoon salt
 10 cups thinly sliced, pared tart apples (Jonathan or
      Golden Delicious)
  2 Tablespoons lemon juice
 1½ cups coarsley chopped walnuts
 12 phyllo-pastry leaves (found in freezer section)
  ½ cup butter, melted

In large bowl, toss sugar with flour, cinnamon, nutmeg and salt; mix well. Sprinkle apples with lemon juice. Add apples and nuts to sugar mixture; toss gently to combine. Set aside. Preheat oven to 375°.

Brush one pastry leaf lightly with butter. Arrange in a 10" pie plate. Layer seven more leaves, brushing each with butter. Turn apple filling into pastry lined pie plate.

Arrange a pastry leaf over filling, brush lightly with butter. Layer on top three more leaves, brushing each with butter. With scissors, cut a 3" wide circle from center of top crust.

Trim edge all around, leaving a 2" overhang. Fold overhang under; form into an edge all around. Bake 50 to 60 minutes, or until apples are tender and crust is golden. Serves 8.

Eastman's Orchard, Donna Eastman, Goreville, IL

Dainty Apple Pie

This is my mother's recipe, used since 1940.

  3 cups sliced Golden Delicious apples
 2½ cups canned grapefruit juice
  1 9" graham cracker pie shell
  ½ cup sugar
  3 Tablespoons cornstarch
      whipped cream
  8 maraschino cherries, chopped

Cook apples in grapefruit juice until tender; remove from juice and arrange in pie shell. Mix sugar and cornstarch, add to juice and cook until clear and thickened. Pour over apples. Cool. Cover with whipped cream and sprinkle with cherries. Store covered in refrigerator.

Doc Carey Homestead Orchards, Onalee Carey, Atlanta, MI

Apple Crumb Pie

5-7   *large, tart apples*
1   *9" unbaked pastry shell*
1   *cup sugar, divided*
1   *teaspoon cinnamon*
¾   *cup flour*
⅓   *cup butter*

Pare apples; cut in eighths and arrange in unbaked pie shell. Sprinkle with ½ sugar mixed with cinnamon. Mix remaining sugar with flour; cut in butter until crumbly. Sprinkle over apples. Bake at 400° for 40 minutes or until apples are tender. Serves 6-8.
Colonial Orchards, Shirley Damm, West Paris, ME

Variations
1. Patricia Oliphant, of Oliphant Orchard in Sherwood, OR adds an interesting twist: Reduce sugar to ⅔ cup. When alternating layers of apples and cinnamon sugar add ½ cup chocolate chips after the first layer. At the end of the cooking time, sprinkle ½ cup chocolate chips on top of pie and bake 5 minutes longer. Patricia suggests serving with vanilla ice cream. She calls it "Johnny Appleseed Pie."
2. Ellen Parker of Parker's Orchard, Millington, MI suggests making a deep dish crumb pie in a 9"x13" pan. She adds cloves to her spice mixture and uses a buttery pastry made with an egg.
3. Annette Smith, Uncle John's Cider Mill, St. John's, MI, suggests using a graham cracker crust and baking the pie in a microwave oven. Cook on High for 14 minutes, turning once. Also, putting a piece of waxed paper under plate while cooking, helps with clean-up.

Apple Brown Betty

1 cup whole wheat bread crumbs
½ cup wheat germ
3 Tablespoons butter
4 unpeeled Winesap or Cortland apples
¼ cup brown sugar
½ teaspoon salt
¼ cup raisins
½ lemon juice and rind

Mix together bread crumbs, wheat germ, butter. Core and slice apples. Add brown sugar, salt, raisins and mix. Fill oiled casserole in alternate layers of apple mixture and crumbs. Sprinkle top with lemon juice and rind. Bake at 375° for 30 minutes covered and 10 minutes uncovered, or until apples are soft. Serves 6.
Academy Gardens, Inc., Wilma Jean Thiry, Elburn, IL

Mom's Apple Cobbler

½ cup (1 stick) butter or margarine
2 cups sugar
1½ cups water
½ cup shortening
1½ cups sifted self-rising flour
⅓ cup milk
1 teaspoon cinnamon
2 cups finely chopped apples
    butter

Heat oven to 350°. Melt butter in a 13"x9"x2" inch baking dish or sheet cake pan. In saucepan, heat sugar and water until sugar melts.

Cut shortening into flour until particles are like fine crumbs. Add milk and stir with fork only until dough leaves the side of the bowl. Turn out onto lightly floured board or pastry cloth; knead just until smooth. Roll dough out into a large rectangle about ¼ inch thick.

Sprinkle cinnamon over apples; then sprinkle apples evenly over dough. Roll up dough like a jelly roll. Dampen the edge of the dough with a little water and seal. Slice dough into about 16 slices, ½ inch thick.

Place in pan with melted butter. Pour sugar syrup carefully around rolls. (This looks like too much liquid, but the crust will absorb it.) Bake for 55-60 minutes. Makes 8 servings.
Hazel Lacy, Campbellsville, KY

Apple Cobbler

        6   cups sliced McIntosh or Spy apples
       ⅓   cup brown sugar
       ⅓   cup white sugar
        1   teaspoon cinnamon
            butter

Topping
      1½   cups baking mix*
        3   teaspoons melted shortening
        1   egg
       ½   cup milk

Mix apples, sugars, and cinnamon in a 9"x13" pan. Dot with butter. Combine baking mix, shortening, egg and milk. Batter should be consistency of heavy cake batter. Drop by spoonfuls over fruit. Bake 15 minutes in preheated 400° oven. Reduce temperature to 350° and bake until fruit is done, about 30 minutes. Serves 8.

*or substitute 1½ cups flour, 1½ teaspoons baking powder and ¼ teaspoon salt

Vogt's Orchard, Helen Vogt, Jackson, MI

Variation
Michelle Ferrante of Wallkill View Farm, New Patte, NY sent a very similar recipe, but she melts ½ cup butter in the baking dish, then spreads in a batter, made from all ingredients except apples, and puts apples on top. Bake about 45 minutes at 350°.

50

Apple Crisp

4   cups sliced, pared, tart apples (Jonathan, Melrose or Winesap)
⅔   cup packed brown sugar
½   cup flour
½   cup uncooked quick oats
¾   teaspoon cinnamon
¾   teaspoon nutmeg
⅓   cup butter or margarine, softened

Heat oven to 375°. Grease square 8"x8"x2" pan. Place apple slices in pan. Mix remaining ingredients thoroughly. Sprinkle over apples.

Bake 30 minutes or until apples are tender and topping is golden brown. Serve warm and, if desired, with light cream or ice cream. Serves 6.

A&M Farm, Alice Adae, Midland, OH

Apple Bread Pudding

2   cups of cubed bread (day old)
4   cups milk (scalded)
2   eggs
½   cup sugar
½   teaspoon salt
1   teaspoon vanilla
½   cup butter or margarine, melted
2   Cortland or McIntosh apples, peeled and sliced
½   cup chopped walnuts
½   cup raisins

Place cubed bread in a bowl, pour scalded milk over bread and allow to become well soaked and slightly cool. Beat eggs only until mixed. Add sugar, salt and vanilla to eggs. Stir into bread mixture.

Add melted butter and stir. Grease a 2-quart baking dish and pour in pudding. Add Cortland apples, walnuts and raisins; stir together. Set dish in a pan containing 1" hot water and bake in a moderate oven of 350° for 60 to 75 minutes or when knife inserted in middle is not too wet. Serves 10-12.

Cross Orchards Roadside Market, Phyllis Cross, La Grangeville, NY

Frosted Apple Bars

Crust

2½	cups flour
1	teaspoon salt
1	cup shortening
1	egg yolk, plus milk to make ⅔ cup

Filling

2	handfulls crushed cornflakes
8-10	Jonathan or Wealthy apples, peeled and sliced
1	teaspoon cinnmamon
1	cup sugar
1	egg white whipped with fork

Glaze

1	cup powdered sugar
1	Tablespoons water
1	teaspoon vanilla

Mix crust in order given, divide dough into two parts. Roll out one part to fill a 9"x13" pan. Sprinkle crust with crushed corn flakes.

Arrange apples evenly over crust; sprinkle with cinnamon and sugar. Roll out remaining crust, place on top of apples. Pinch edges. Brush top crust with beaten egg white. Bake at 400° for one hour. Remove from oven and frost with glaze while warm. Serve warm with a fork or cool and cut into bars. Serves 10-12.

Note: Oven temperatures vary. If the top is getting too brown, reduce heat to 350°. Also, depending on the type of apples used, you may need to bake only 40-45 minutes.
Schwenker's Orchard, Gerri Schwenker, Rochester, MN

Variations
1. Evie Ostendorf, J&R Provisions in Cedar Falls, IA uses rice crispies if cornflakes aren't available, and she flavors the glaze with 1 Tablespoon butter, 2 Tablespoons warm milk and ¼ teaspoon almond flavoring instead of water and vanilla. Evie uses a combination of Granny Smith, Red Rome and Johnathan apples.
2. Nita Gizdich, Gizdich Ranch, Watsonville, CA uses Newton Pippins or Golden Delicious in her "Nita's Apple Squares." She also dots the apple mixture with ½ cube butter prior to putting on the top crust.

continued on next page

3. Mrs. Ray Holt, Holt's Orchard in Edna, KS uses Jonathans or Winesaps. Her dough is a bit different. She uses:

2	cups flour
½	cup sugar
½	teaspoon salt
½	teaspoon baking powder
1	cup oleo
1	egg, beaten

Mrs. Holt presses one-half of the dough in a 13"x9"x2" pan, adds 6 medium sliced apples, tossed with ¾ cup sugar, ¼ cup flour, and 1 teaspoon cinnamon. Then she crumbles the rest of the dough over top. (A different appearance and slightly different flavor combination.) Can drizzle with powdered sugar icing if more sweetness is desired.

4. Mrs. John McIlquham of Chippewa Falls, WI calls this "Apple Jack" and likes to make it with McIntosh Apples. She notes that it keeps well.

Chocolate Applesauce Cake

1½	cups flour
¾	cups sugar
¼	cup cocoa
1	teaspoon soda
½	teaspoon salt
1	cup applesauce
½	cup cold water
⅓	cup oil
1	teaspoon vanilla
1	Tablespoon vinegar

Sift flour once and add all dry ingredients. Then sift all together again. Add rest of ingredients. Blend in bowl until all is moistened. Pour into a greased and floured 8" square or round pan. Bake 35 to 40 minutes at 350°. (For a 9"x13" cake or double layer cake, just double recipe.)

This cake is moist enough to eat unfrosted, or good with your favorite buttercream frosting.

Moore Orchards, Beth Peters, Hood River, OR

Apple Walnut Coffee Cake

3   eggs
1   cup cooking oil
2   cups sugar
3   teaspoons vanilla
3   cups flour
1   teaspoon salt
½   teaspoon baking powder
1   teaspoon soda
¾   teaspoon nutmeg
3   teaspoons cinnamon
2   cups chopped apples
1   cup chopped walnuts

In large bowl beat eggs, add cooking oil, sugar, vanilla and cream together until fluffy. Add dry ingredients, mixing well. Add apples and nuts. Stir to evenly distribute.

Put in greased and floured bundt pan. Bake in a 300° oven for 45 minutes. Increase heat to 325° and bake 20 minutes longer.

Let cake cool 15 minutes. Remove from pan.

Cox Orchard, Nancy Cox, Cleveland, MN

Variation
Marietta Hodgens of Hodgen's Orchard in Rainsville, AL sent a similar recipe and added this delicious topping

¾   cup brown sugar
½   cup shredded coconut
½   stick margarine or butter
½   cup nuts
¼   cup milk
½   teaspoon vanilla

Mix sugar, milk and butter. Bring to a boil. Add nuts, vanilla and coconut. Pouru over cake as soon as it is removed from pan.

Fresh Apple Cake

2	cups sugar
¾	cup salad oil
2	eggs
2	Tablespoons vanilla
2	cups flour
1½	teaspoon baking soda
1	teaspoon salt
2	teaspoons cinnamon
4	cups chopped Gravenstein, Golden or Jonathan apples
1	cup chopped walnuts

Cream sugar and oil; add eggs and vanilla and beat again. Add flour, soda, salt, and cinnamon sifted together. Add apples and nuts. Pour into ungreased 8½"x13½" pan. Bake 45-55 minutes in 350° oven. Cool. Serve with whipped cream, or frost with:

Frosting

8	ounces cream cheese
1	stick margarine or butter
1	box powdered sugar
2	Tablespoons vanilla
	chopped walnuts

Cream cheese and margarine. Add sugar and vanilla and beat thoroughly. Frost cake and top with chopped walnuts. Serves 18.
Riverland Ranch, Joyce Carver, Corvallis, OR

Variations
1. **Maple Lawn Farms, New Park, PA** sent a very similar recipe; they suggest adding raisins rather than nuts to cake batter.
2. **Pat Marshall, Marshall's Apple Farm, Sebastopol, CA** sent a similar recipe for which she also suggested Granny Smith apples. She said the recipe makes good cupcakes.
3. **Molly Papenheim, of Victoria Valley Orchard, St. Paul, MN** uses Haralson apples. She recommends mixing all ingredients with a spoon, and baking in a greased and floured 9"x13" pan. Molly suggests a caramel topping: Combine ½ cup butter, 1 cup brown sugar, and ¼ cup evaporated milk in a saucepan. Bring to boil, and maintain a gentle boil for 2½ minutes (count carefully). Pour hot topping onto cooled cake.

Apple-Date Cake

Moist and delicious.

        1   cup chopped Wealthy or Jonathan apples
        1   cup chopped dates
        1   teaspoon baking soda
     1½   cups sifted flour
        1   teaspoon salt
        1   cup boiling water

Combine ingredients. Cover with 1 cup boiling water, and set aside to cool.

        ½   cup shortening
        1   cup white sugar
        1   egg
        1   teaspoon vanilla
        ½   cup chopped nuts

Mix shortening, sugar, egg and vanilla together, alternately add date and flour mixture and chopped nuts. Bake in a 9¼x13" pan, at 350° for 50 minutes. Serves 12.

Cream Cheese Frosting
        1   cup powdered sugar
        3   ounces cream cheese
        4   Tablespoons margarine
        1   teaspoon vanilla

Drizzle over cooled cake. May add milk to make a drippy frosting.
Alpine Orchards, Mrs. Janice Schweitzer, Comstock Park, MI

Apple Spiced Cake

3¼	cups sifted flour
2½	cups sugar
¾	cup butter or margarine, softened
3	eggs
2	teaspoons baking soda
1½	teaspoons salt
½	teaspoon ground nutmeg
½	teaspoon ground cinnamon
6	cups pared coarsely chopped Stayman or Winesap apples
2	cups chopped walnuts

Orange Rum Syrup

2	teaspoons grated orange rind
½	cup orange juice
¼	cup sugar
¼-½	cup rum

Preheat oven to 350°. Combine first eight ingredients in large mixing bowl; mix at low speed until well blended. (Mixture will be very dry.) Add apples, 1 cup at a time, mixing well after each addition. Stir in nuts; turn into well greased and floured bundt pan or 10" tube pan. Bake 1 hour and 15 minutes, or until toothpick comes out clean. While still hot, drizzle syrup over top until absorbed.

Orange Rum Syrup: Combine all ingredients in small saucepan. Bring to boiling, reduce heat and simmer for 10 minutes. Drizzle over hot cake. Can be served with whipped cream, or plain as coffecake. Serves 16.

Gobbler's Knob Orchard, Rose Auker, McAlisterville, PA

Variation

Mrs. John Phillips, Carrie's Apple Stand in Red Creek, NY sent a similar recipe, but she uses 2 teaspoons cinnamon, 1 teaspoon vanilla and baking powder instead of soda in her cake. She bakes it in a 9"x13" pan. Also, you can reduce nuts to 1 cup and add 1 cup raisins.

Glazed Fresh Apple Cookies

"This has been in the family for 75 years."

4½	cups flour
1	teaspoon clove
1	teaspoon nutmeg
2	teasapoons cinnamon
1	teaspoon salt
2	teaspoons soda
1	cup shortening
2⅔	cups brown sugar
2	eggs
1	cup cider*
2	cups finely chopped appled, unpeeled (Ida Red or Jonathan)
1	cup raisins
1-2	cups nuts

Sift together flour and spices. Cream shortening and brown sugar. Add eggs, cider and chopped apples. Add dry ingredients, fold in raisins and nuts. Drop from spoon on greased cookie sheet. Bake at 375° for 10 minutes. Glaze while hot and remove from pan.

Glaze

1	Tablespoon butter
1½	cups confectioner's sugar
⅛	teaspoon salt
2½	Tablespoons cider*
¼	teaspoon vanilla

Cream butter, sugar, and salt. Stir in apple juice and vanilla.
*Can substitute orange juice or milk for cider (if cider unavailable). Don't use vanilla when using orange juice!
"Farmer" Bayne's, Patricia Bayne, Freeland, MI

Apple Torte

2	cups flour
1	cup shortening
1	Tablespoon sugar
⅛	teaspoon salt
18	Wealthy or Cortland apples
1½	cups sugar
1	teaspoon cinnamon
4	egg yolks
2¼	cups milk
6	Tablespoons sugar
2	Tablespoons cornstarch
	salt
4	egg whites
½	cup sugar

Mix flour, shortening, sugar, and salt until like pie crust—no water—just crumbly. Line bottom of pan and sides of a 9"x13" cake pan. Pat mixture down.

Fill pan with sliced apples, mix sugar and cinnamon and pour over apples. Bake 1 hour at 350°. A cookie sheet may be put over apples to steam them while they bake. Take out of oven and start custard.

Beat egg yolks until thick; add 2¼ cups milk, sugar, cornstarch, salt and cook until thick. Cool, then pour over apples. Beat egg whites till stiff, add sugar, pour over custard and brown at 350°. Cool. Serves 18.

Rabideaux's Orchard, Allen & Mary Jo Rabideaux, Bayfield, WI

Chocolate Apple Tea Muffins

¼ cup butter
¼ cup sugar
1 egg
2 cups sifted cake flour
½ teaspoon salt
3 teaspoons baking powder
1 cup milk
1 square (1 ounce) unsweetened chocolate, melted
½ cup grated apples

Cream butter. Add sugar while continuing creaming. Add egg and beat well. Mix and sift flour, salt, and baking powder, and add alternately with milk to the butter mixture. Stir in chocolate and apples.

Spoon batter into well-greased small muffin pans (2 inches top diameter), filling ⅔ full. Bake at 375° for about 25 minutes. Remove from pans, cool on racks.

If desired, split muffins; spread one side with whipped cream cheese, the other with currant jelly and put back together. Makes 24 small muffins, great for guests or lunch box surprises.

Freeze ahead if desired before splitting for filling, or simply dust tops with confectioners sugar. The flavor of chocolate is not over-powering, and compliments the slightly tart winey flavor of the apples in a most delightful way.

Maple Lawns Farm, New Park, PA

Apple Pizza

2 Tablespoons flour
½ cup firmly packed brown sugar
1 teaspoon cinnamon
1 can refrigerator biscuits
2 cooking apples, peeled, cored and grated
1 cup grated mild cheese
   dab of butter

Measure the flour, sugar and cinnamon into a small bowl. Mix well. Press or roll biscuits into flat circles and place on a lightly greased cookie sheet. Sprinkle grated apples on biscuits, then sprinkle with grated cheese. Spoon on brown sugar mixture and dot with butter. Bake at 350° 15-20 minutes.

Peaches 'N' Cream Farm, Helen Lamb, Seymour, MO

Apple Delight

Crust

1¼	cups flour
1	teaspoon salt
½	cup shortening
1	cup shredded cheddar cheese
¼	cup ice water

Filling

½	cup powdered non-dairy creamer
½	cup brown sugar
½	cup sugar
⅓	cup flour
¼	teaspoon salt
1	teaspoon cinnamon
½	teaspoon nutmeg
¼	cup butter
6	cups Spy or Golden Delicious apples, sliced
2	Tablespoons lemon juice

Crust: Blend first 3 ingredients until crumbly; add cheese. Sprinkle water over and stir until dough forms. Roll to fit 15"x10"x1" pan. Push dough up sides.

Filling: Combine dry ingredients. Sprinkle ½ over crust. Cut butter into remaining mixture until crumbly. Set aside for topping. Arrange apple slices over crust. Sprinkle with lemon juice, then cover with crumbs.

Bake in preheated 450° oven, 30 minutes. Serve warm, plain, with ice cream or whipped cream. Serves 15.

Dutch Acres, Joyce Kayim, Allegan, MI

Apple Pancake

2   medium tart apples
2   cups flour
3   Tablespoons sugar
1   Tablespoon baking powder
½   teaspoon salt
½   teaspoon cinnamon
1⅓   cups milk
½   teaspoon vanilla
3   Tablespoons butter
     brown sugar
     maple syrup

Preheat oven to 450°. Peel, core and thinly slice apples. In mixing bowl combine flour, sugar, baking powder, salt, cinnamon. Add milk and vanilla, mix until smooth.

Melt butter in a 12" oven proof skillet. Arrange apples in bottom of pan and pour batter over.

Bake until apples are golden, about 15 minutes. Turn by flipping pancake over onto a plate, then sliding it back into the pan. Continue baking until other side is golden and pancake is cooked through. About 10-15 minutes.

Remove from pan, sprinkle with brown sugar and serve with maple syrup.

Martina Boudreau, Editor, St. Louis, MO

Microwave Apple Pie

1   9" graham cracker crust
5-6 sliced Ida Red, Spy, Cortland or McIntosh apples
1   Tablespoon lemon juice
½   cup sugar
2   Tablespoons flour
½   teaspoon cinnamon

Topping

½   cup margarine
½   cup flour
¼   cup brown sugar
½   teaspoon nutmeg

Mix apples, lemon juice, sugar, flour and cinnamon and put in pie crust. Mix all ingredients for topping together and put on top of pie. Put wax paper under plate while cooking. Microwave on High power for 14 minutes turning once.

Uncle John's Cider Mill, Annette Smith, St. John's, MI

Gingerbread 'n' Apples

2	cups sifted flour
1	teaspoon cinnamon
1	teaspoon ginger
½	teaspoon cloves
¼	teaspoon salt
½	cup shortening
1	cup sugar
1	egg, well-beaten
3	Tablespoons molasses
1	teaspoon soda
1	cup buttermilk or sour milk
1½	cups tart apples diced (Stayman or Golden Delicious)

Pre-heat oven to 350°. Mix and sift together flour, spices and salt. Set aside. Cream shortening; add sugar gradually and cream until soft and fluffy. Add egg and molasses. Beat well.

Dissolve soda in milk. Add milk and flour mixture alternately to creamed shortening and sugar, beating well after each addition. Stir in diced apples.

Bake in a well-greased floured cake pan (9" square) at 350° about 50 minutes until gingerbread pulls from sides of pan. Serve warm with dollops of sour cream, yogurt or whipped cream. Serves 8.

Mountain Green Farm, Sally L. Sharp, Washington, VA

Crunchy Apple Dessert with Brandy Sauce

1½	cups baking mix
1	cup sugar
1	egg
3	medium McIntosh or Cortland apples
½	cup walnuts
2	Tablespoons melted butter or margarine
1	Tablespoon sugar
½	teaspoon cinnamon

Sauce

¼	cup sugar
2	Tablespoons baking mix
1	cup natural apple cider
1	Tablespoon butter or margarine
½	teaspoon brandy extract

Heat oven to 350°. Grease 8"x8"x2" pan. Mix first three ingredients until crumbly. Lightly press ⅔ of this mixture into pan. Top with 3 apples, coarsely chopped, and walnuts. Sprinkle butter over top. Mix remaining sugar and cinnamon and sprinkle over all. Bake until golden brown (about 35 minutes).

Serve with Apple Brandy Sauce:

Mix sugar and baking mix in 1 quart saucepan. Stir in cider and butter. Heat to boiling, stirring constantly. Boil, and stir, one minute. Remove from heat and stir in brandy flavoring. Serve warm. Serves 9.

Scholl & Sons Orchards, Irma Scholl, Richland Center, WI.